The Almond Tree

Also by Bill Dodds:
a novel *Twisted Lives*

The Almond Tree

Bill Dodds

Published by ATQUE

Copyright © Bill Dodds 2010

Bill Dodds asserts the moral right to
be identified as the author of this work.

ISBN: 978-0-9559871-1-3

This work is a product of the author's imagination.

All rights reserved.
No part of this publication may be reproduced,
stored in a retrieval system,
or transmitted, in any form or by any means,
electronic, mechanical, photocopying, scanning,
recording or otherwise, without the prior permission
of the author.

A catalogue record for this book is available from the
British Library.

For Karine Polwart

Acknowledgements

Many thanks to Karine Polwart for allowing me to include her poem *THREE*, by way of preface to the collection.

Thanks to the editors of the following publications in which some of these poems first appeared: *Monkey Kettle, Cannon's Mouth and Inclement.*

Contents

THREE	i-iii
Eden	1
Psyche	2
Ambition	3
Illusions	4
Blinded Doge	5
Master of Death	6
Serenissima	7
Haircut	8-9
Wallpaper	10
First	11
May I?	12
The mill pool	13
Rose hip	14
The briar	15
Breathe	16
Red	17
Once	18

The troubadour	19
The border parish	20-21
Natural selection	22
The gift	23
Anima	24
His sole desire	25
The sea	26
An eighties girl	27
Future imperfect	28
The abstract society	29
The departure	30-31
Spectral echo	32
Arrival	33
Water mirror	34
Smile	35
Hermitage	36
Chaos theory	37
Belle époque	38

The nativity	39
The rose	40
Beauty	41
The fire	42
Edouard Manet	43
Fragmentary dream	44
The almond	45
My darling	46
The pilgrim	47
Saint Héloise	48
You came	49
It does	50
Questions	51
Notes	52

THREE

1.
The first voice has an almost giggle
in it, as it always has.
A nervous flutter sounding like it might have done
when it was
breaking
first
forty years ago and more.
Bewildered.
And in between.
It does not know how the words should fall on this
occasion,
so as not
to say
what remains
to be said.
It adds, "This sounds strange"
And it does.

The second voice is broken.
Clean.
Politely crushed.
It was not always so.
Never a voice to say too much
too fast,
it tells me,
please,
what I should do.
It would be most obliged.

2.
Strange news is come to this door
Strange news and stranger still
In boots and a bobble hat I hap you up from the morning chill

One brother makes another call
And one brother lets it ring
At the head of the path you laugh as a lone blackbird begins to sing

Strange news arrives unbidden
Strange news and stranger still
There are plastic strings of gold and ice cold beer on the windowsill

A mother does just what she must
And a father comes undone
In the not yet snow we wave and shout hello to a welcome sun

Strange news is at this table
Strange news and stranger still
There's glitter on the dirt road, a light slung low on the hill

Somewhere a boy is asking when
And somewhere a woman why
In the field out back we wait for the crack of wings in a winter sky

3.
By the river where the woods walked
you stalked a beam of light upon a bough
and caught it,
luminous and green,
not evergreen.
I know this now.

For EP

Karine Polwart

30 December 2008

The Almond Tree

Eden

A power pointed dour refrain,
of stubborn words, rehearsed but blank,
empty my hapless, hopeless mind
of peering crowded faces, in which
one smile, a face I recognise, unguarded
I smile back, should I have done that?

The undergraduate glances
at the shaded court outside,
tastes the whisky of ideas, where
acrobatic words vault, twist, and tumble,
phrases of slurred intellect that shout,
stubborn imperative, no doubt?

Bemused roots drag my feet to earth,
cold clay surrounds my trunk, and numbs
to sleep my calves, my thighs, my loins.
Clenched fists beat at a tightening chest
of shortening breath, until senseless,
I am expelled from Eden.

Psyche

My lover,
Melancholia.

Extended glad hands,
Wrenched from Cupid's grasp.

Breezy greetings,
Lost amidst silent calls.

Sensual smiles,
Shrouded in midnight's snarl.

Amorous kisses,
Exiled beyond desolate oceans.

Sweet perfumes,
Engulfed by rancid breath.

Loving caresses,
Transformed to ironstone touch.

A sentient being,
Shrivelled into nothingness.

Melancholia,
my lover.

Ambition

Bewildered, northern star
tends her windswept garden.
Lost, mere mortal dreams
dim her radiant star.

Illusions

A small boy dreams about

Becoming
his heroes
his dad
his dad's heroes
his own heroes.

Overcoming
his heroes
his dad
his dad's heroes
his own heroes.

Escaping
his heroes
his dad
his dad's heroes
his own heroes.

Capturing
his heroines
his mum
his mum's heroines
his own heroines.

Losing
his heroines
his mum
his mum's heroines
his own heroines

A small boy dreams about
lions, tigers, and elephants.

Blinded Doge[1]

No eastern silks, no lustrous satins wrap his corpse,
a carcass purged of filth, stripped naked now,
skin stretched tight, arms cross jutting ribs,
jaw gapes, tongue lolls, last perfumed breath exhaled.

No ducal diadem, but crowned with plundered thorns,
soiled hands, washed feet, nailed to splintered rood,
guile, pride, holy wisdom desert him,
supplicant, he waits, fears final judgement.

No priests guide him, no slaves support his faltering path,
winged lions roar, inflame the faithless crowd
of devils, gawping, spitting spiteful prayers,
crowing demons hail an empty tomb.

Hands tremble, legs stumble, toes test the ladder,
angels avert their gaze, Saint Peter turns his back,
first step breaks, his body drops through time,
his graceless fall, fiends applaud, welcome his proud soul.

Master of Death[2]

Seven years dead,
not to the day,
a day of deaths,
my mum, Mike
a date close by,
Phoebe[3] rekindles
the warm embers,
unconscious,
she invokes,
scholarly irreverence,
carnival, charivari,
a nun rambles,
picks a penis
from the phallus tree.

Serenissima

Carnival has begun.

Serenissima smiles,
walks the square mile
face hid by papier mask,
clad in fools' gold.

Serenissima smiles,
lutes charm his ears,
ring fingers entwined,
dances risk's tune.

Serenissima smiles,
eyes gleam at twilight,
pledges vast lust,
grabs mercury coins.

Serenissima smiles,
lies on her back,
implores quick release,
tricks innocent buyer.

Carnival is over

Serenissima smiles,
kneels to the priest,
confesses her sins,
mocks a new penance.

Serenissima smiles,
hides in the shadows,
bares her whore's breast,
attracts a new client.

Carnival never ends.

Haircut

Through the window,
two faded jeans
busy quick cutters,
remove my coat on entry,
scan the local's ads,
glance at lads' Sun,
turn to my thoughts,
she beckons,
my regular Miss.

To her chair,
body?
youthfull,
hair?
blonde and black,
eyes?
unnoticed hue,
snip, snip, snip,
my regular Miss.

Zombies to each other,
she begins, speaks,
her normal chat up line,
day off? – she says,
write – I say,
at home, kids, wife who
works four days a week,
more to say, to others,
my regular Miss.

Plans for today? – she asks,
post a birthday card to Oz,
Junction, Cambridge, a gig,
Oh? Eating out?
more dead phrases,
sad ends of word,
glasses returned,
mirror shows
my regular Miss.

Side burns trimmed,
fringe widowed,
back tapered neat,
not too short,
brushes, fusses,
passes tissue,
says farewell,
she smiles, okay,
my regular Miss.

Wallpaper

The plastic film repels the heat,
melts and stretches,
defeated,
off it comes,
more paper to remove.
people I muse,
outer layer hides truth,
persevere?
peel over days months years,
more texture underneath,
rough prisoners escape,
mimics of inner-selves,
less sure, more absorbing,
thoughts come quicker,
if one has pushed that far,
not slapped a neutral coat of paint,
not papered over the remains of carcinoma,
not moved to another room,
too much effort?
too much scalding steam?
yet her skin falls away,
revealing,
her smooth flesh,
herself alone.

First

Wise pupils, greedy for her,
swirling hips, paradise unseen between,
senses unknowing, beguiled beneath,
half imagined hazy dreams,
of she who fades before the robber sun.
Too hasty gaze betrays the naked soul,
stripped bare of silence, dazed,
wary, but past pretence, impatient
his mind can not escape the nervous smile,
given once, twice, too many times to be
politeness wrapped in silly teasing jokes,
sex in mind, that grander game that adults play,
with nervous teenage steps they hide, one, two,
three, ten, twenty, coming , ready or not.

May I?

Recorder, drum, fiddle, claps and shouts,
music quickens, heartens dancing steps,
gnarled, proud, maypole summons, beckons,
dizzier, dizzier, circle spins, minds glow,
Sir Priest stamps his feet, eyes up a buxom girl,
parents, sons, daughters, faster, faster,
wrap the maypole, garland with spring flowers,
colours white, yellow, green, lover's perfume,
crimson faces of old, regain their youth,
cry *la volta*,[4] lift partners, stumble towards
church house, sit, watch, gossip, drink ale
before sad couples part, lovers slip away,
desires woven in darkness, cloak lust,
 shroud love's beginning and its end.

The mill pool

She swims,
lover of the old mill pool,
Apollo's golden gaze,
her leaden nakedness,
fingers tangle in horn-wort's leaves,
strokes ripple the calm meniscus,
palms brush jealous minnows,
soles caress smooth pebbles,
in the shallows,
Daphne clambers,
sloughs her skin,
rests, sun dried,
on care worn mossy bank,
pools, where forebears lay,
cool water at fiery sunset,
she washes over him,
purifies his lust,
bathes his love,
he swims.

Rose hip

An unselfish lover,
forgives, embraces
a conceited soul,
mirada fuerte.[5]

A ripe rose hip is
pomegranate's ward,
the delight of earth's garden,
with her crimson black mandala.

He presses fecund flesh,
sucks her sweet syrup,
spits out her hard seeds.

The briar

Honeyed reprimand for tearing out
those rampant briars,
that threatened rambling rose,
barbed black spike protrudes,
stabbed through brittle husk,
hooked deep into his flesh,
painless unless he prods and pokes,
ventures to extract, with stainless steel,
pricks with dirt clad finger nails,
squeezes at the burglar's roots,
wait, be patient, skin mends,
surrounds her with a bitter pus,
membrane blisters, fractures,
expels the briar.

Breathe

Blasted phrase conveys,
premature ejaculation,
from work's fetid womb,
banished to life's margins.

Monastic contemplation,
wrestled with ludicrous,
masked fenland forms,
eye of bat, ear of corn.

Peroxide-blonde pills,
bleached darkling thoughts,
exiled joy and despair,
displaced imaginings.

Discontent, my man-fate,[6]
spewed those cruel pills,
ate cold turkey until I felt
creation's breath upon my lips.

Red

Red light exists,
out there, selfless,
seven centuries
of nanometres,
give or take
intensity of shade.

In space not time,
excited neurons,
spark positive charges,
as serotonin jumps,
across synapses' salty gaps,
to construct perception.

Same place, next time,
he will see red,
she will see red.

Red's quality lives,
in here, selfish,
that rakish, raffish colour,
love's shadow, lust's bonfire,
gives and receives
passionate sensation.

Within consciousness,
vigorous phenomena,
shake mind's trees,
with tempestuous storms,
open his eyes to her eyes,
awaken intimate desires.

Same place, next time,
Will he want her?
Will she want him?

Once

We wore crazed masks,
behind puzzled smiles,
expressed glazed phrases,
fired by serious,
complicated minds,
late evolved to study,
modern continental greats,
yet ill-adapted to survive life's
random thunder-claps,
then, all loved-up, we
smashed our masks,
scattered the falsehoods,
like our own cremated ash
amongst the fallen berries
of the churchyard yew.

The troubadour

Tambourine held high,
beating time's selfishness,
breathed chivalric love songs,
langue d'oc,
langue d'oeil,[7]
desire indifferent,
Cathar perfection,
Christian redemption,
claps, strokes her bird of prey,
strapped to her thigh, silken flesh,
blind hooded beast,
gentle as its lady's tongue,
she lusts,
her arrows tipped with neither
flint nor steel, but flesh,
his corrupted male flesh.

The border parish

The rector yawned, rubbed his eyes, blinked.

He hugged his fox fur close and stared across the field mi
that danced half a man high, into the yellow light of horn
glazed lamps, flames shuddering in shaken gloved hands,
uplifted as in *Benedictus benedicat*, his clerical square hat
hugged his ears, muffled the shout, but his clerk heard,
and was gone and the bell tolled in passing the tide.

The rector did not pray, not right then.

He admired the velvet black drape, white crosses in silk,
shouldered by two reivers, father and son he knew, evil
North Tyne men. Half a dozen behind, woollen cloaked,
hooded helmets, jacks proofed for musket balls, targes
strapped to padded thighs, bows unstrung, bills weeping
droplets condensed from hot breath on cold blighted stee

The rector did not pray, too frightened.

The cortege wavered past the rector, into south porch,
his leather soled slippers slid on church tiles, where riding
boots had shed the crimson streaked moss waters, four
candles alight at each corner of the parish coffin, perched
open on the bier, lined with a woollen shroud, the corpse
poured into space like pregnant rye before a threshing.

The rector did not pray, curious now.

Her eyes cornflower blue stared, auburn hair raped
from its pins and bows, a cream linen cap hung loose
untied beneath her chin, her mouth a crimson circle of
swollen shredded lips, tongue rage-blackened by fingers
red-marked around her throat. Keening women circled him,
bearing a clean smock, water pails, dried herbs and flowers.

The rector prayed, he prayed for her soul.

Genuflected to the Mother, climbed the steps,
spiralled to the platform, where he attended to the Rood,
dusted His wounds and lit great larded lumps of candles,
those black faced sheep[8] paid well with their flesh and
fleece, into his chamber, sight fired by Whickham coals,
his clerk munched brown seeded bread, drank small beer.

The rector opened the leaded pane, he drank moonlight.

He heard the shriek, heard the laughter,
he saw the shadow man stretched, clawing at the rope,
kicking his heels from the bough of the red berried yew tree,
eyes staring at the leaden crucifix,
ears straining for words of absolution,
in purgatory until death plucked out his soul.

The rector did not pray, he wept Christ's tears.

Natural selection

Today litter picking duty, six pounds,
each hour a bag full of twenty fag-end
crisp, sweet and sour, condom, mars-bars,
strewn round the green organic bench,
that overlooks the village green.

Open grave cut's future is predestined,
elect, unlike her current tenants, defleshed
one hopes, shoved to one side by a box,
veneered in plywood, all souls to wait
for judgement's band, when bones
will dance the Morris.

Five teenagers occupy the bench,
school's out in half an hour,
'chavs' my daughter calls them,
three boys, two girls, well dressed in
trainers, jeans, the lads dart around the
yard, dodging dad's headstone, spitting
gum, one lad trips, the others laugh, turn,
the girls are gone.

The gift

Linguistic ability, his prized possession,
scholar, hunter of a rainbow princess,
through Homer, Virgil, to modern masters,
on whom he doted, whilst his mind churned
bellicose language, sentences of hate-crammed
propaganda in a just war, fought in obscurity
for marxists, monarchists, fascists, bastards all,
he wrote often, love letters, she studied herself,
and wrote him, so and so, dishonest nothings,
she spurned bad faith, told him of her conquests,
bellowed her existential freedom,
no chaste pretence, no fiery hearth for his return,
bullets killed him, abandoned, assassinated,
his parents' gift to her, his bloodstained Catullus,
by return, on receipt of her considerate condolences.

Anima

Three playing cards,
cut from the stack.

Twisted by sly painted
lady, face down naked.

Flee, the queen of daylight,
blue-eyed, buxom, bonnie.

Spurn, the princess of the night,
dark business suit, slim and sexy.

Choose, the mistress of my mind,
stern, sad, sage and silent. Be still.

His sole desire

He once yearned to wear her shoes,
those blackened playful dancing pumps,
toes scuffed and torn, heels snagged,
his sole desire, caress her naked dent,
that dead remnant of teenage years,
she wears spiked heels today, gloss black,
leather, the price ambition paid, with
failed lovers the reward she wrought,
and he no longer worships her, for he
wore the pumps, and touched her soul.

The sea

We all do it, shameless, ugly,
sea beasts, inspired by salted
pride, too often unconcerned
by feckless strokes of bloated life,
specious, forced human waves,
that overwhelm weak swimmers
against the deluge, and we are,
are all weak swimmers, fallen,
scraped caricatures from some
utopian bestiary, left over from
a plundered Spanish galleass,
the Barbary sea spurns us all,
too soon, resents disturbance
to its calm replacement of each
lunar tide, our petty will to rule,
supreme, it spits us out, onto
a violent, pebbled beach, alone,
skin blistered, spirit decomposed.

An eighties girl

Eyelids fluttered as if she still dreamed night-marred
fantasies of an eighties girl, age nineteen, university,
new freedom from her parents, whose settled petit
bourgeois life of six AM to ten PM, small mortgaged
northern semi, tasks broken by sex and slumber,
concealed behind locked bedroom door, betrayed
by hasty stifled gasp, occasional pleasured curse,
she screamed for feminism regained, longed for
cataclysmic lovers, life unthreatened by pregnant
pauses, a well paid London job, a weekend cottage,
Her degree, Oxford, life ensnared by a worthy House,[9]
five minute coffee walk from one bed basement flat,
laboured six AM to PMT, stroked male bosses' pride,
entertained in town clients, sniffed powdered darkness,
club 'til one AM, when latch keyed, dreamless she slept.

Future imperfect

Too busy with the plastic mirror,
hair straightener in sweaty hand,
mascara, blusher not yet applied,
to buy the look, cool conformist,
to the modish times, afraid, death
to be excluded, a geek or goth,
young adult anguish rules the heart.

More complex later years, united
or divided by the books we read,
political opinions, music, class, sex,
headstrong in our gastric ghettos,
of old friends, normal restaurants,
dressed like the people we were,
once, before our children followed.

Don't cross those lines then darling,
walk it, talk it, love it, snort it, fuck it,
why stretch out? lean over fences?
those borders of petty self delusion,
sad self determination, hold back then,
annihilate the present, make the future
imperfect and live in the past tense.

The abstract society

Once upon a time, anxious for the clunk,
of printed matter, brown A4 envelope,
content devoured with restless stare,
pornographic, featureless articles, he
read, and thought he knew the names,
believed in them, advocates for their
own dim egos, stars in adversarial letter
pages, searchers for nonplussed offices,
at home in Gulliver's worlds, these the
abstract society, until dates of publication
forgotten, the unloved envelope, sealed,
lumped with free newspapers, pages
uncaressed by fingers, unkissed by eyes,
direct debit cancelled, membership
secretary keen to know the reason why,
no pictures? too few features? no news?
No use to him, those voids of names, words
stripped of flesh and bones, dried sinews,
withered muscles, cold as frozen corpses,
tongue-less, death dancers, no use to him,
not as he is, nor as he will be, no use at all.

The departure

Yesterday the carer nodded,
unlocked the numbered door,
assured us of integrity,
regretted disinfectant,
wished us well, no rush.

Five years past she,
read the Mirror,
watched Corrie on ITV,
two black plastic bags,
folded, laid on the one
stripped naked bed.

Four years gone-by she
recognised the kids,
smiled and joked,
old worn clothes
in the wardrobe,
wasted keep-sakes
in the chest of draws.

Three years now she
asked when will they
be home for tea,
an inlaid box,
a wedding ring,
a press report
of his demise.

Two years ago she
spoke his name,
wanted him to take her
to the Grafton Rooms,[10]
suit-cased photos
of the mourned,
husband, mother
brother.

Last visit daughter
kissed her mum,
those chapped
lips enquired,
'When's the next bus
to Wavertree Clock?[11]
Where am I?
Who am I?'

Spectral echo

See cavernous chairs gather,
surround beer slopped tables,
bitter, mild mildew, mixed,
false stucco, ornamental gilt,
pissed, arts and crafts urinals.

Not here?

Imagine once, the stage door
johnny, a friend tonight, working
our boys and girls, bevied up,
eyed up, duffel-coated strangers,
students past the bombed church.

Not there?

Stare at sailors, whores and pimps,
befriend commercial cellar bars,
suited bankers, insurance clerks,
solemn Somme bound Liverpool Pals,
toast their drink sodden remembrance.

Nowhere?

Wander the Dock Road, redundant,
Liver birds shit on cruel tenements,
God she shadows him, consumptive,
down alleys to the slave dark river,
mud, sinking sands glad hand him.

Gone.

Arrival

Accidental arrival or destiny's shifty shrug,
straight black pathway, down, hell bound,
moon fleshed, shadowed steps, ghosts,
attractive ghouls of past subtle entrancers,
shallower waters than tonight, tunnelled
sight of whitened floor, lion-clasped gate,
beehive chamber, guarded, glanced forward
towards her dais, three thrones, musicians,
silence, dialectical procession, far distant,
glimpsed murmured movement, closer,
face flashed out, disembodied head,
lime silver, powdered cheeks, sparkle,
glitter, scattered sunset red, expectant,
mouths betray her sex, blacked out eyes,
mindless, possessed of another, man, god,
listless paces flow, nearer, a hand's width,
open eyes dance, bared breasts, snake bitten.

Water mirror

Chiselled channels, smudged fey shadows, lines,
charcoal over lead white uplands, flint marred
a handsome face, a savage smile of recognition,
hesitant, hidden by her baulk, turned sad towards
a downward tunnel, entrance to the Styx, he mused,
fleeting steps went, away into absence, last scattered
memories of her billowing skirt, her bitten back words,
his slaughtered questions, his dreams arrived unasked,
unbidden he followed, slain by new confusions,
her empty silhouette, a higher caste, colour of sunset's
attempted sunrise, of twisted woollen threads, a skein,
woven with golden wire, numinous, taught disturbance
to settled surface dust, ahead a slight rise, right several
dozen foot-beats, hearth flames, a lambskin covered
chair, unsheathed bed, water mirror, he stares until
the snake goddess appears, and beckons his reflection.

Smile

He abandoned the myth, sheltered by the lithic canopy,
the path spiralled, tightened, she wrapped her limbs around
his voided personality, he desperate for her truth, scratched
nail deep, bare-fisted, he entered a corridor of painted walls,
impressed by oil dipped sullen cords, daughters of faltering
radiance, near death flames, ancient and modern threads
of intertwined desire, her steps quickened, eyes screwed
acrobatic dancers, male and female, naked bull leapers,
watched by his goddess, her captured snake spat venom,
he hissed, squirmed, demanded release, but she refused,
denied escape, he gulped cold air, roughed wet sand,
smelt salt and smoking flesh, heard the waves foam,
beheld her, and imagined the shades of her smile.

Hermitage

Skirted the mill, sailed across fielden paths,
barefooted, skipped seeded thistles, hems
snatched, sparrow hawk hovered, nude
abandoned hinterland beyond the corn,
deserted fish days' ponds, deep black silt
over once fertile water meadow, ditch
drained, smocks dragged over unpinned
hair, skirts slipped down quickened hips,
toes deep in skin cold river mud, floating,
arms outstretched to grasp a reeded bank,
an island, hawthorn rooted ramparts, red
raw, scratched intruders in a sacred place
of stones, knelt, tumbledown, as one, still
unready, unlearnèd, mouthing the letters,
chiselled, *haec porta coeli est*,[12] stammering
a ritual of marriage, written not for them.

Chaos theory

Predictive
futility,
like fertility,
as instinctive,
yet,
I don't know,
you don't guess,
probability's farce,
is bell shaped,
least squares'
c h o
     it
          ac
consternation,
but
determined to be
the mathematical
         noise that
wobbles the world
of shadowy orgasm,
    add
a random
        mortal emotion,
double doubt,
find oneself
 a philosophical question
is she in love?

Belle époque[13]

The bearded man,
he daydreams away
his herbal *déjeuner*,
now *la jeunesse*
ignores the picnic,
shuts his ears, hears
no friendly gossip,
for inside that head,
a nymph bathes, and
comes naked to enjoy,
with him, a simple reverie.

The nativity

Across the forest path,
a woman, laid out, straight,
dressed in Sunday best,
a fresh faced corpse, neat
black shoes against virgin
white hose, legs tensed,
tight, pushed together,
a hand protects her belly,
a fist supports her head,
birch trees project her glory,
silver summer sunlight kindles
her still-born, native sexuality.

The rose

Winter's darkness savages
Eve's earthly garden,
defeats the scorching sun's
exposure of frightened shivering souls,
whose eyes grip one another,
distanced by a failure of the will.
Eh bien, le coup de foudre
annihilates all that was before,
uproots tear-stained lily of the valley,
but finds red rosebuds scrambling free.

Amoureux, heureux.
Amoureuse, heureuse.

Beauty

A smile of yellow, ground down teeth,
cigarette squeezed in blackened fist,
metaphorical smoke stings his eyes,
cheapened perfume distends his nose,
the shadows clear, the sun shines,
a bright smile of love appears for once,
to sing and dance within his sallow soul.

The fire

Her sight, her singeing lips,
a summoner offering pardon,
a respite from purgatory.

Her distance, her insatiable gaze,
a leash of exquisite silken hope,
a devastating monastic kiss.

Her retreat, a backward glance,
a coy lifting of a muse's veil,
an invitation to attend her flame.

Edouard Manet

A barmaid all outward show, no modesty,
to tempt the dapper *fin de siècle* gentleman,
all dressed in black, mourning beard, top hat,
Madame at home, contemplating modern art,
decoration, impressions of poppies, poplars,
our *bourgeois gentilhomme*, shifts left, judging
his reflection, leaning on his syphilitic stick, sips
numb death, this year, gangrene, amputation,
unconscious, nothingness, from being Manet.

Fragmentary dream

Passionate, deft sensual signings,
unheard, sight more intense
than hum-drummed sexy words,
proscribed by hell's fire storms,
a scalding circle of hissing poison,
kissing tongues, crazed prophetic,
mimics of the other self, the one
darling mouthing frantic fantasies,
daring formless disembodied lust
to love, escape from her cindered flesh.

The almond tree

Its fruit,
velvet,
crushed,
green skin,
flesh,
blushed red,
rain blessed,
lips opened
by the searing sun,
let slip,
a pitted carapace,
the past,
fallen,
to grace,
a winsome path,
snatched,
by a preying bird,
a seeker,
soared,
sunset bounden,
dropped,
smashed,
exposed,
the kernel,
devoured
the creamy flesh.

My darling

I've watched the wings,
gilding blackened clouds,
shrouding golden sunrise,
chiding maddening sunset,
how long now, my darling?
decades of sleepless nights?
years of paralysed days?
I hear its cold shriek, close,
close now, perched, a branch,
spiked talons, scimitar fangs,
seducer's eyes bind mine,
an inert corpse sunk in earth,
head suffocated by a pillow,
soft feathers, the vulture's own.

The pilgrim

His crazy, hazy mind a shifting maze,
a labyrinth of cluttered weed strewn
paths, where knots of subtle words
stumble like wanton travellers once
devoted to a medieval saint, holy
signed by a leaden scallop shell,
lit by a fiery wheel, the pardoner
sells indulgence for fewer weeks
of waiting, languishing in purgatory,
a drab's habit, a monk's black hood,
clothed masked forms that flicker, dim
beyond the shadows, forever tempting
the pilgrim to another wayside shrine,
at which to pray, one more mass illusion,
before death summons him to dance.

Saint Héloise[14]

Somewhere obscure,
cathedral town,
chaste nunnery,
cherished bones wait,
encased in gold,
cloisonné work,
engorged lip-red,
pale virgin blue.

Pilgrim rejoice,
kiss her sainthood,
revive her desires,
joyous bare feet,
trample moist grass,
naked bodies
on flaxen sheets,
her new lover,
safe within her.

You came

Quickened, her step falsetto,
one extended hesitant stride,
chewing gum jaws, blanched
cheeks, blackened eye lids,
glanced downwards, twice.

Unfathomable those big boots,
smart calf high, zebra striped
leather, rouged laces tied taut,
bowed, as a scribbled unread
signature, but the hook, ahead
a shaded look undressed him.

He pretended, walked casual-like,
crossed his arms, closed around
his chest, he clocked those boots.

'You came,' she spoke,
as if he'd spooked
her conscious brain.

A boot paced nearer,
each grinned, hugged.

It does

Peers in twilight,
drizzle,
gloom,
illuminated ghosts,
made it,
pleasured,
measured voices,
apparitions are we?
familiars,
face-down
improper forms,
mould complex acceptances,
step back,
shared,
given,
even-handed,
clown-like,
coucou,[15]
subdued subterranean
streams,
dreams,
flow
arise
causal,
of unique acts,
flood the mourning moon,
drown the wintry sun,
life flickers,
next day,
it dawns,
it does.

Questions

The wise man counsels.
Ask only questions:
To which I know the answer.

The wise woman senses.
Evade the questions:
To which I know the answer.

Evaded questions,
Hear us crow.

Unspoken questions,
Nail our Cross.

Sic transit gloria mundi.

Notes

[1] The blind Doge was Enrico Dandalo, who directed the Fourth Crusade that sacked Constantinople and imposed Latin rule.

[2] Mike Camille, friend and scholar, 1958 to 2002, an expert on the medieval world.

[3] Phoebe in Greek mythology a daughter of Uranus and later associated with the moon, the huntress and prophecy.

[4] An Elizabethan dance in which the man lifted his partner.

[5] *Mirada fuerte* is a fierce sexual stare associated with Picasso painting and Andalucia.

[6] See William Everson *Man-Fate*, 1974.

[7] The *langue d'oc and langue d'oeil* were the languages of southern and northern France respectively in medieval and early modern times.

[8] In early modern England sheep were kept to pay for specific church candles or lights.

[9] House: a reference to a City firm, which referred to themselves Houses because of their Oxbridge and public school connections.

[10] A dance hall popular in Liverpool before the Second World War.

[11] James Picton built the Wavertree clock tower in 1884 as a memorial to his wife Sarah Pooley.

[12] Literally: here is the entrance to heaven.

[13] See Manet's painting *Dejeuner sur l'herbe*.

[14] This poem was provoked by the visit of the relics of St. Thérèse of Lisieux in 2009; revered for doing small acts with great love.

[15] *Coucou:* common French for hello.

www.ingramcontent.com/pod-product-compliance
Lightning Source LLC
Chambersburg PA
CBHW071416040426
42444CB00009B/2270